One of my favourite Easter traditions is the Easter egg hunt. Admittedly, as I hide the chocolate eggs for my children, I do surreptitiously enjoy a few myself.

But a couple of years ago, it was a very different kind of Easter hunt that made the news. Twenty years before, two of Charles Darwin's notebooks had been stolen from the University Library in Cambridge. One of them contained his famous drawing of his "Tree of Life", outlining his theories of evolution. Above the sketch, he had written two words:

I think.

What does that have to do with an Easter hunt? Well, because over two decades later, the notebooks reappeared at Easter time outside the head librarian's office, in perfect condition, in a pink gift bag. Along with the notebooks was a printed note, reading:

Librarian: Happy Easter. X.

The hunt had lasted 20 years, and then suddenly it was over. But who had taken them, where they had kept them, why they had wanted them and why they had returned them... all that remained a mystery.

Another Mystery

A hunt and a mystery. That was the theme of Easter 2022 for the University Library in Cambridge. It was also the theme of the very first Easter. At its heart was a man who had healed the sick and walked on water and raised the dead. Some had started to think he might be God himself, living in the world he'd made. But then this man, Jesus, had been arrested and executed — killed by being hung up on a wooden cross and then placed in a tomb in a garden. At that point it was all over. Until, three days later...

> *Early on the first day of the week, while it was still dark, Mary Magdalene went to the tomb and saw that the stone had been removed from the entrance. So she came running to Simon Peter and the other disciple, the one Jesus loved, and said, "They have taken the Lord out of the tomb, and we don't know where they have put him!"*
>
> (The Gospel of John from the Bible: chapter 20, verses 1 to 2)

The hunt was for a man who had been dead but whose body had disappeared. The mystery is that the writer, an eyewitness of the events called John (who calls himself "the other disciple"), claims that Jesus had risen from the dead. That claim lies at the heart of the Christian message — but it is hard to believe. Dead people don't rise from the dead!

Yet that is what millions of people today believe happened on that particular day to that particular man. And that's another mystery — that so many people believe something so unlikely. I'm one of them — and here are three reasons why I think that such a seemingly unbelievable claim is actually true...

1. The Absence of a Dead Body

> *So Peter and the other disciple started for the tomb. Both were running, but the other disciple outran Peter and reached the tomb first. He bent over and looked in at the strips of linen lying there but did not go in. Then Simon Peter came along behind him and went straight into the tomb. He saw the strips of linen lying there, as well as the cloth that had been wrapped round Jesus' head. The cloth was still lying in its place, separate from the linen. Finally the other disciple, who had reached the tomb first, also went inside. He saw and believed.* (John 20:3-8)

No one (if Jesus hadn't risen back to life) has ever adequately answered the question of where Jesus' body went.

Imagine you were one of Jesus' enemies (he had a lot of powerful ones), and you had taken the body from the tomb for security reasons. When people started talking about his apparent resurrection, you would have produced the body to prove them wrong. But no one ever did.

Or imagine you were a grave robber, and you'd taken the body. Wouldn't you have also taken the only thing of value in the tomb – the grave clothes? But they were left behind when the body disappeared. When John reached the tomb that morning, he saw them – and to him, they were like the discarded chrysalis from which a butterfly had emerged. He saw them – and he started to believe that Jesus had risen.

2. The Presence of a Living Man

Mary stood outside the tomb crying. As she wept, she bent over to look into the tomb and saw two angels in white, seated where Jesus' body had been, one at the head and the other at the foot.

They asked her, "Woman, why are you crying?"

"They have taken my Lord away," she said, "and I don't know where they have put him." At this, she turned round and saw Jesus standing there, but she did not realise that it was Jesus.

He asked her, "Woman, why are you crying? Who is it you are looking for?"

Thinking he was the gardener, she said, "Sir, if you

have carried him away, tell me where you have put him, and I will get him."

Jesus said to her, "Mary." (John 20:11-16)

Mary was not expecting to see Jesus alive. Even when he spoke to her, she assumed he was the gardener. But when Jesus said her name, she began to realise that the impossible had happened. And it wasn't only this one woman who saw Jesus alive after he'd died...

On the evening of that first day of the week, when the disciples were together, with the doors locked for fear of the Jewish leaders, Jesus came and stood among them and said, "Peace be with you!" After he said this, he showed them his hands and side. The disciples were overjoyed when they saw the Lord. Again Jesus said, "Peace be with you! As the Father has sent me, I am sending you." And with that he breathed on them and said, "Receive the Holy Spirit." (John 20:19-22)

Mary could, of course, have been hallucinating. But these disciples — at least ten people — saw the same thing at the same time. (And a few weeks later, 500 people would see him at the same time — 1 Corinthians 15:6.) Group hallucinations simply don't happen. And so these other disciples also started to believe that Jesus had risen.

3. The Transformation of the First Disciples

These first followers of Jesus were, by their own account, trembling "for fear of the Jewish leaders". Then something happened, and just weeks later they were proclaiming to thousands that "God has raised this Jesus to life, and we are all witnesses of it" (Acts 2:32). When those same religious leaders threatened them and arrested them, instead of trembling with fear they insisted that they had seen Jesus alive after he'd died. Over the next few decades, almost all of the people who claimed they'd seen the risen Jesus that first Easter Sunday proved willing to be killed rather than keep quiet about what they said they'd seen. What a transformation! What caused it?

Chuck Colson was Special Counsel to President Nixon and was part of the Watergate scandal back in the 1970s. He was jailed for his part in the conspiracy to cover up a politically motivated burglary. While he was inside, he became a Christian – he came to believe that Jesus had risen. He wrote:

> "I know the resurrection is a fact, and Watergate proved it to me. How? Because 12 men testified they had seen Jesus raised from the dead, then they proclaimed that truth for 40 years, never once

denying it. Every one was beaten, tortured, stoned and put in prison. They would not have endured that if it weren't true. Watergate embroiled 12 of the most powerful men in the world — and they couldn't keep a lie for three weeks. You're telling me 12 apostles could keep a lie for 40 years? Absolutely impossible."

So What?

It's these three strands of evidence — the absence of the dead body, the presence of the risen Jesus, and the transformation of his followers — that have persuaded so many people that the mystery of the hunt for a dead man was actually solved by the surprising fact that Jesus really did rise from the dead on that first Easter Sunday. In fact, it was those three strands of evidence that persuaded me too, 30 years ago at the age of 17.

But there's more. Because, if the answer to "What happened on the first Easter Sunday?" is "Jesus rose from the dead", that raises a second, even more important question: so what? What difference does that make today? For me, aged 17, coming to recognise that Jesus had risen from the dead was the catalyst for changing my whole outlook on life. As a teenager, I thought that God probably didn't exist, but that, if he did, he was a killjoy out to spoil my fun. However, when I saw that Jesus had risen from the dead, I put my trust in him as my Lord and Saviour, and began to discover the great news that God was not a killjoy, but my perfect heavenly Father, who wanted what was best for me.

Here are three reasons that I discovered as to why Jesus rising from the dead is great news...

1. Pardon for Your Past

Recently, I met a woman on Clapham Common, near where I live in London. She was kneeling on the grass, crying. We got talking, and she told me that she was furious with life because she was furious with herself – that she had done things that made her a terrible person. The root of her anguish was that she believed that her past could not be pardoned. She felt stuck in guilt.

Jesus' friends knew that feeling. In the 72 hours before the events of the first Easter Sunday they had abandoned him, failed him, broken their promises to him. Yet when the risen Jesus met with them, his first words were "Peace be with you". It was his way of saying *I forgive you.*

Our past can be pardoned. Our guilt can be removed. Before Jesus rose, he died on the cross to take the guilt and the punishment we deserve for rejecting God. Ultimately, our rejection of God's rule is the wrong that lies behind all our other wrongs – a rejection of Jesus' rule in our lives. That's what the Bible calls sin, and we are all guilty of it. Yet

Jesus, God himself, came to die to pay the price of our sin on the cross, and to rise to say "Peace be with you" to people burdened by guilt like that woman I met, and to people like me and people like you.

I remember reading about a man whose young daughter was crying in their garden. She was being chased by a bee, so he ran to his daughter and wrapped his arms around her. Moments later she felt his body tense. Then he let her go, saying, "You don't need to worry anymore – the bee has stung me, and bees can't sting twice".

We all deserve to face the sting not of a bee but of death and judgment because of our sin. But on the cross, it is as though Jesus wrapped his arms around us and took the sting for us, in our place, so that we need never suffer it. "It is finished," he announced, just before he died (John 19:30). We do not need to remain weighed down by our shame, our despair, our sin. There is complete pardon available for our guilt if we seek it from Jesus. It's the most wonderful experience of freedom. It's what I experienced when I was 17, and it's what I spoke about to the woman I met on the common.

2. Power in Your Present

The same day that I met that woman, I happened to meet another woman, who lived on the same street as me. She was very different: wealthy, successful, together. When she discovered I was a vicar, she told me she wasn't religious. But she also told me she was keen to tend to her soul. She was desperately looking for a power to be at work in her. She was into positive thinking, mindfulness and yoga exercises, and had been going through a book of miracles that promised to transform her as a person.

She was looking for power to live well, power to change, power to overcome. And one way or another, I think most people are looking for that kind of power to help them through life. Those first disciples knew the real source of that kind of power because Jesus had told them about it when he met them as they were trembling with fear on that first Easter Sunday. "Receive the Holy Spirit," he said to them. Jesus himself gives the power that we need. As one of Jesus' first followers, Paul, put it:

> *[God's] incomparably great power [is at work in] us who believe. That power is the same as the mighty strength he exerted when he raised Christ from the dead.* (Ephesians 1:19-20)

The same power that God the Father used to raise Jesus his Son from death to life is available to every follower of Jesus. There's no other power like that, and in Jesus we can experience that power in the present, enabling us to live well, to change, to get through the hard times.

3. Peace about Your Future

"Peace be with you" is an offer not just for today but for eternity – for life beyond death.

We don't much like to think about death. But it's the only real certainty of life. Sooner or later, we will have to confront it. Does it bring to an end all we've worked for and hoped for, including all the relationships we've enjoyed and the love we've known? Not if Jesus rose from the dead. If he rose from the dead, then we can too – there is a way to avoid an eternity without anything good and look forward to a life of perfection with him that never ends.

I have a friend who once decided to visit a Death Café. I didn't know they existed – but apparently, you go along, drink tea, eat cake and discuss death. "Our aim," said the blurb, "is to increase awareness of death to help people make the most of their (finite) lives". The aim is to try to help people get over their natural aversion to death by talking about it and accepting it. So my friend went along, and during the discussions, he mentioned that, as a Christian, he had a hope and a peace about death because Jesus had got through death himself and so would get him through too.

The café organiser was decidedly irritated that my friend was bringing his Christian worldview into the conversation and tried to get him to be quiet. But before my friend could be "cancelled", another person sitting in the group spoke up:

"I don't know about you, but" – and he pointed at my friend – "I just want what he's got".

Wouldn't it be great to have an assurance about death and what lies beyond? To know that, however this life goes for you, there will be better days ahead and one day all your difficult times will lie behind you? That's what the risen Jesus offers you – peace about your future, even your future beyond your death. As Jesus' follower Paul put it, "We believe that Jesus died and rose again, and so we believe that God will bring with Jesus those who have fallen asleep [that is, died] in him" (1 Thessalonians 4:14). Surely, if there is anyone you want to be holding on to as you die it is someone who has got himself through death and so can get you through death too.

The Real Tree of Life

Why can we solve the mystery of the first Easter Sunday with the answer "Jesus is risen"? Because there was no body, because Jesus appeared, and because his followers were transformed. And why does Jesus' resurrection make a difference? Because he offers pardon for your past, power in your present and peace about your future. That's the reason Jesus came at the first Easter. That's the reason why it matters for you and for me.

How do you take up Jesus' offer? By looking at a very different "Tree of Life" to Charles Darwin's. Look at the wooden cross on which Jesus died – a tree on which he hung to offer you forgiveness and eternal life.

Darwin wrote "I think" above his sketch. Jesus invites you to say "I trust" about his tree, because that's all you have to do. There's no need to go on some long, convoluted hunt to take up the offer. You simply need to trust that his death and his resurrection are where you can find pardon, power and peace. You can express that now, using the words of this simple prayer:

Lord Jesus

I am sorry for all the ways I have rejected you in the past — in my attitudes and my actions.

I thank you that you came to this world in love to die in my place. Thank you that death could not hold you and that you rose from the dead and are alive today.

Please come into my life by your Spirit so that I may know your pardon for the past, your power for the present and your peace for the future.

Thank you that you are the best one to guide me through life and through death.

I trust in you.

Amen.

What actually happened at the first Easter? And why does it even matter?

"Here's a mystery – right now millions of people around the world believe that on a particular day in history, a dead man called Jesus rose back to life. Not only that, but they think it's great news for them and for their futures today. And I'm one of the people who think all this is actually true..."

Discover three reasons why this seemingly unbelievable claim might really be true – and three ways that this event could make a huge and wonderful difference to you this Easter.

Jago Wynne *is the Rector of Holy Trinity Clapham in south London.*

thegoodbook.com | .co.uk

ISBN 978-1-80254-276-9

Holidays / Easter & Lent